baby bullfrogs

spoonbills

starlings

For John and Milo

The children featured in this book are from the Luo tribe of south-west Kenya.

The wild creatures are the Citrus Swallowtail (butterfly), Striped Grass Mouse,
Yellow-headed Dwarf Gecko, Beautiful Sunbird, Armoured Ground Cricket,
(young) African Bullfrog, African Spoonbill and Superb Starling.

The author would like to thank everyone who helped her research this book,
in particular Joseph Ngetich from the Agricultural Office of the Kenya High Commission.

Text and illustrations copyright © 2002 Eileen Browne
Dual Language copyright © 2003 Mantra Lingua
This edition published 2003
Published by arrangement with Walker Books Limited
London SE11 5HJ

British Library Cataloguing in Publication Data:
a catalogue record for this book is available from the British Library.

Published by
Mantra Lingua
5 Alexandra Grove, London N12 8NU
www.mantralingua.com

CR
P
BRO

مرغ هندا

Handa's Hen

Eileen Browne

Farsi translation by Parisima Ahmadi-Ziabari

mantra

مادر بزرگ هندا یک مرغ سیاه داشت.
اسم او مُندی بود- و هر روز صبح
هندا به مُندی صبحانه میداد.

Handa's grandma had one black hen.
Her name was Mondi - and every morning
Handa gave Mondi her breakfast.

یک روز مُندی برای گرفتن غذایش نیامد. "مادربزرگ!" هندا صدا زد. "مُندی را جایی دیده اید؟"
"نه" مادر بزرگ گفت." امّا من دوست تو را می بینم."
"اکیو!" هندا گفت . " کمک کن که مندی را پیدا کنم."

One day, Mondi didn't come for her food. "Grandma!" called Handa. "Can you see Mondi?"
"No," said Grandma. "But I can see your friend."
"Akeyo!" said Handa. "Help me find Mondi."

هندا و اکیو اطراف مرغدانی را گشتند.
"ببین! دو تا پروانه که دارند پرواز می کنند،" اکیو گفت.
"امّا مُندی کجاست؟" هندا گفت.

Handa and Akeyo hunted round the hen house.
"Look! Two fluttery butterflies," said Akeyo.
"But where's Mondi?" said Handa.

با دقت زیر انبار غلات را نگاه کردند.

"ش ُش ش ُ! سه تا موش با خط‌های راه راه،" اکیو گفت.

"امّا مُندی کجاست؟" هندا گفت.

They peered under a grain store.

"Shh! Three stripy mice," said Akeyo.

"But where's Mondi?" said Handa.

آنها پشت چند کوزهٔ سفالی را با دقت نگاه کردند.
”من چهار تا مارمولک کوچلو می بینم،“ اکیو گفت.
”امّا مُندی کجاست؟“ هندا گفت.

They peeped behind some clay pots.
"I can see four little lizards," said Akeyo.
"But where's Mondi?" said Handa.

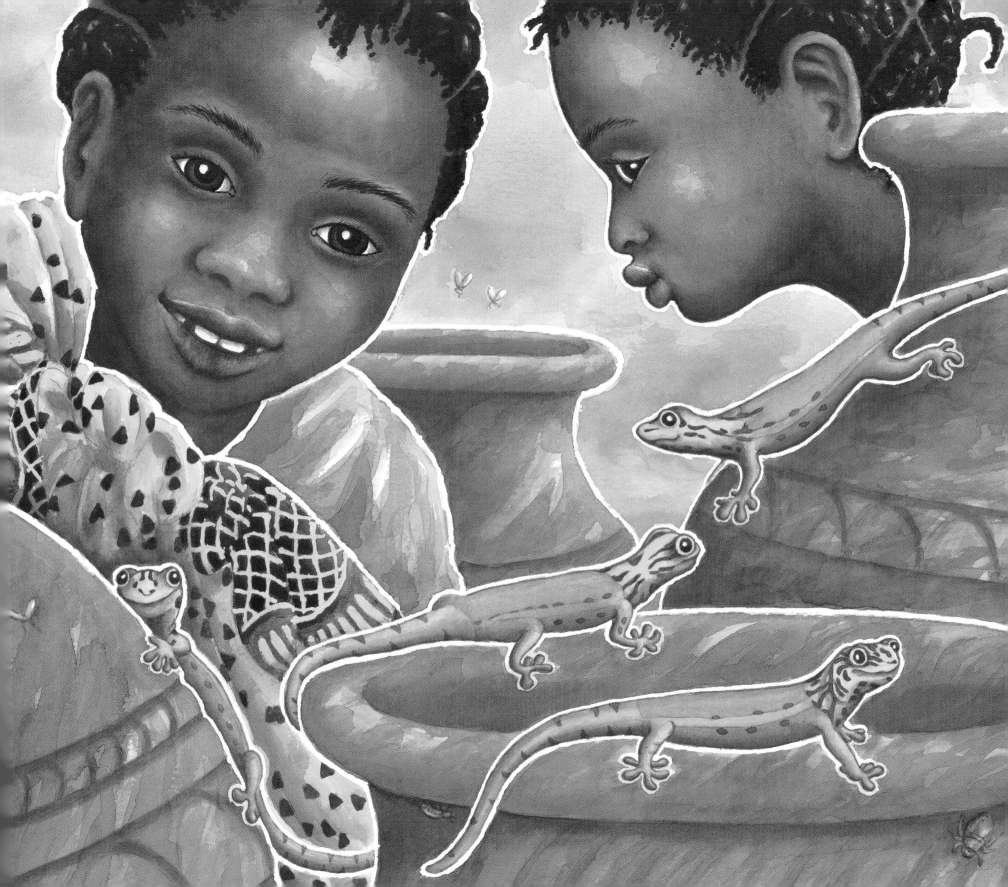

آنها اطراف چند درخت پُر گل را جستجو کردند.
”پنج تا پرندهٔ زیبای سینه سرخ،“ اکیو گفت.
”امّا مُندی کجاست؟“ هندا گفت.

They searched round some flowering trees.
"Five beautiful sunbirds," said Akeyo.
"But where's Mondi?" said Handa.

آنها در علفهای بلند و موّاج نگاه کردند.
"شش جیرجیرک که می‌جهند!" اکیو گفت. "بیا آنها را بگیریم."
"من می‌خواهم مُندی را پیدا کنم،" هندا گفت.

The looked in the long, waving grass.
"Six jumpy crickets!" said Akeyo. "Let's catch them."
"I want to find Mondi," said Handa.

آنها به داخل چالهٔ آب رفتند.

"بچّه غوک ها،" اکیو گفت. "آنها هفت تا هستند!"

They went all the way down to the water hole.
"Baby bullfrogs," said Akeyo. "There are seven!"

"امّا ... اُووو نگاه کن! ردّ پا!" هندا گفت.
آنها ردّ پا را دنبال کردند و فهمیدند ...

"But where's … oh look! Footprints!" said Handa.
They followed the footprints and found …

‟فقط مرغ سقا،“ هندا گفت. ‟هفت تا … نه، هشت‌تا.
امّا کجاست، وای مُندی کجاست؟“

"Only spoonbills," said Handa. "Seven … no, eight.
But where, oh where is Mondi?"

"امیدوارم مرغهای سقا اورا نبلعیده باشند-
یا یک شیر او را نخورده باشد،" اکیو گفت.

"I hope she hasn't been swallowed by a spoonbill -
or eaten by a lion," said Akeyo.

با غمگینی، آنها پیش مادر بزرگ برگشتند.
"نُه تا سار درخشان – آنجا هستند!" اکیو گفت.

Feeling sad, they went back towards Grandma's.
"Nine shiny starlings - over there!" said Akeyo.

"گوش کن،" هندا گفت. چیپ‌چیپ "آن صدای چیه؟"

چیپ‌چیپ چیپ‌چیپ چیپ‌چیپ چیپ‌چیپ

"از زیر بوته ها می آید. می‌خواهی یواشکی نگاه کنیم؟"

"Listen," said Handa. cheep
cheep "What's that?"

cheep   cheep   cheep   cheep
cheep   cheep   cheep   cheep

"It's coming from under that bush. Shall we peep?"

هندا، اکیو، مُندی و ده تا جوجه

Handa, Akeyo, Mondi and ten chicks

با عجله خیلی سریع به خانهٔ مادر بزرگ برگشتند.

hurried and scurried and skipped back to Grandma's …

در آنجا همه با هم یک صبحانهٔ دیر خوردند.

where they all had a very late breakfast.

hen

mice

lizards

butterflies

sunbirds

crickets

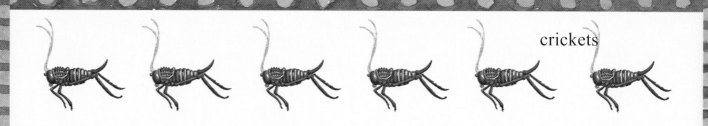

baby bullfrogs

spoonbills

starlings

chicks